T0131632

CHANGE—JUST DO IT

Productivity Training Kit Cum OSP
Business Strategy Card Game

ROBERT TEH KOK HUA

BALBOA.
PRESS

A DIVISION OF HAY HOUSE

Balboa Press books may be ordered through booksellers or by contacting:

Balboa Press
A Division of Hay House
1663 Liberty Drive
Bloomington, IN 47403
www.balboapress.com
1 (877) 407-4847

Because of the dynamic nature of the Internet, any web addresses or links contained in this book may have changed since publication and may no longer be valid. The views expressed in this work are solely those of the author and do not necessarily reflect the views of the publisher, and the publisher hereby disclaims any responsibility for them.

The author of this book does not dispense medical advice or prescribe the use of any technique as a form of treatment for physical, emotional, or medical problems without the advice of a physician, either directly or indirectly. The intent of the author is only to offer information of a general nature to help you in your quest for emotional and spiritual well-being. In the event you use any of the information in this book for yourself, which is your constitutional right, the author and the publisher assume no responsibility for your actions.

Any people depicted in stock imagery provided by Thinkstock are models, and such images are being used for illustrative purposes only. Certain stock imagery © Thinkstock.

Print information available on the last page.

ISBN: 978-1-5043-3992-6 (sc)
ISBN: 978-1-5043-3993-3 (e)

Library of Congress Control Number: 2015914507

Balboa Press rev. date: 10/27/2015

CHANGE, JUST DO IT
Laws of Nature

For ages, people have been talking about it. It is the ultimate solution to human problems. It holds the secret of success. It is the recipe for peace, harmony and progress. That magic word is change.

Unfortunately change is no magic wand. Nothing much has changed considering the world is basically trapped in the same old inefficiencies, and malpractices, of the past, culminating in wars, conflicts, revolutions, political unrests and financial meltdowns like Asian Financial, US Subprime and Eurozone crises etc. Despite such painful lessons, people seem content to engage in rhetorics about leadership, meritocracy, planning, organizing, creativity, productivity schemes, capital budgeting which have not worked to protect their own vested interests or seek refuge in some comfort zone.

The good news is whether you are a student, housewife, worker, boss, chief executive or government minister, there are ample scientific evidences pointing to the presence of a force or Tao within us to help us achieve our goals and dreams. To begin, you may choose to be positive. By being positive, you will soon be connecting your mind to a force within our being, doing the necessary and possible, the principal secret of success.

The author intends to share with readers a robust relational database execution platform (RDBM) known as Objective-Steps Processing (OSP) that connects the mind to an invisible force or Tao to help us change. It was conceived out of practical necessity while he was working as manager in diverse environments encompassing property/ facility management, foundation piling, construction of oil refinery, dredging, harbour work, transmigration projects, LNG loading docks and operation/maintenance of sea-going vessels and floating cranes or salvage works during the period 1970s-2000s. It has helped him to simplify and standardise tasks and work productively as detailed in the productivity handbook: "Change you can".

Being a condensed version, of the afore-mentioned productivity handbook, this book will focus on the essentials and application aspect of OSP. Because of its robustness, OSP is easily acquired with practice of an entertaining OSP Business Strategy (OBS) Card Game, (on normal 52 playing cards) as explained in Table B in Appendix I. More importantly, it enables people to think and act in oneness with a force or Tao within our being in simple steps namely: (a) laying bare workflow processes to expose hidden relationships (b) motivating the workforce to attain easy-to-recall targets set in mind and matter relationships.

Speaking of laws of nature, it was believed at one time that matter is made of earth, metal, water, fire, air and aether. However by following an atomism approach a process of continuously breaking down the unknown into smaller elements as suggested by Democritus, scientists have finally albeit after some two thousand years of conceptualization, achieved one of the biggest breakthroughs in science - discovery by Robert Boyle that compounds of gas like carbon dioxide can be broken down to their chemically indivisible building-block elements called atoms (read the book "Atom" by Isaac Asimov).

Additionally, the atomism approach, has enabled scientists to unlock secrets of the universe including the following :-

1. Cause-effect law of nature,
2. Conservation of energy,
3. Pair production,
4. Attraction of the opposites,
5. Dark energy permeating the universe.
6. Interactions between force and field to form matter.
7. Einstein's energy-mass equation: $E=MC^2$
8. Contents of universe – matter, dark matter and dark energy.
9. Pauli exclusion principle,
10. Quantum mechanics.

From the afore-stated laws of nature, and other scientific evidences to be elaborated below, we can surmise that the universe is made of energy alternating in binary elemental (+1) and (-1) pulses to form mirror-image matters and anti-matters; clearly the universe is ruled by a mind and matter continuum. Scientists believe that the universe was born in a big explosion from a singularity. No explanation has been given for the Big Bang Theory. However, according to Einstein, the primordial void of space contains a negative pressure. By the laws of physics, such negative pressure indicates presence of a potential energy source. In fact, under the Standard Model of particle physics, it is well established that energy exists as forces and fields interacting in binary (+1) and (-1) elemental states to form matters and anti-matters [(+1)(-1) and (-1)(+1)]. Our heart beats in "on" (-1) or "off" (+1) elemental energy states under the control of an all-pervasive power source in the form of an electrical system called the cardiac conduction system as follows:-

1. **S-A node (sinoatrial node)** — known as the heart's natural pacemaker, the S-A node has special cells that create the electricity that makes your heart beat.
2. **A-V node (atrioventricular node)** — the A-V node is the bridge between the atria and ventricles. Electrical signals pass from the atria down to the ventricles through the A-V node.
3. **His-Purkinje system** — the His-Purkinje system carries the electrical signals throughout the ventricles to make them contract. The parts of the His-Purkinje system include:

   - His Bundle (the start of the system)
   - Right bundle branch
   - Left bundle branch
   - Purkinje fibers (the end of the system)

Furthermore, by the Anderson Cloud Chamber Experiment, a beam of light (photon) from space was found to split into mirror-image pair of negatively charged electron and positively charged positron upon impact with a 6 mm lead sheet in cloud chamber. Clearly such a beam of light is energy (photon) that originated in the primordial void prior to the Big Bang. By the law of electromagnetism, energy interacts as forces and fields deflecting electrons in a direction perpendicular to its motion. During lightning, such forces and fields are routinely converted to existential states of electrons (-1) and positrons (+1). Hence, there exist ample scientific evidences, showing that the universe is ruled by an energy source residing in the primordial void of space alternating in smaller binary energy states of (+1) and (-1) keeping the universe in a state of constant change and us living and alive.

Given the above-elaborated concrete scientific evidences, it is not far-fetched or speculative for Max Planck to observe that matter originates and exists by virtue of a force. We must assume the existence of a conscious and intelligent mind. This mind is the matrix of all matter. It is here that physics and metaphysics begin to overlap. - actually demanding a re-integration of science, philosophy and spirituality in order to fully understand how both our world and we work. Planck explained that "the universal energy or quantum web as illustrated in countless experiments responds or reacts to human thoughts, expectations, beliefs and even emotion. Afterall, thoughts, expectations, beliefs and emotions are really nothing more than another form or expression of the same thing : quantum energy. In other words, our thoughts are essentially connected to everything and everyone that exists in our environment." (Read "The Synthesis Effect" by John Mcgrail).

Other instances of mind and matter continuum include the ability of the first unitary cell of living things to divide itself into similar cell types over time, to form into different organs in its future body at exactly the positions needed serving unique meaningful purposes of lives. Our brains themselves are constructed in a binary left and right pair imparting a Yin and Yang harmony or balance enabling us to think and act in accord with the binary energy laws of nature. Our body is able to produce enzymes to keep us immune from attack by different diseases by intent, specific to addressing the different external attacks.

Looking back, ancient Chinese philosopher Lao Tzu had postulated in his book" "Tao Te Ching" that the universe is ruled by a higher order called force or Tao. Other influential Chinese philosophers Fuxi, King Wen, and Confucius had similarly observed such a higher order manifesting as Yin and Yang harmony of nature. In particular, Lao Tzu had advised people "to live selfless lives in accordance with nature, not to go against the way of things and not claiming greatness, to achieve real greatness" and that "through serving the needs of others, our own needs will be fulfilled", and "after you have attained your purpose, you must not parade your success, you must not boast of your ability", "it is a good sign that a man's higher nature comes forward, bad sign that man's lower nature comes forward". The Tao and Te dualism is akin to the parallel law of meaning postulated by physicist Pauli Wolfgang and psychologist Carl Jung. Dr. Wayne Dyer had observed that the Lao Tzu's thoughts have been the most influential thoughts on human behaviors. (Read "Change Your Thoughts, Change Your lives").

This being a book on change, and not Tao, it suffices to discern the essence of Tao of relevance to change as follows (see David Villano's book "Tao Te Ching", the numbers within bracket refer to reference nos. of the principles):-

(A). The Tao creates all from nothing. It is everywhere. It is the creator of all people and it is everything we can and cannot see. Each person and object is created with perfect balance: weak and strong, soft and hard, silly and serious. Without balance, we are doomed: An arrogant man may lose his friends; a violent man may die in a violent death. All things come and it and return to it. It is always within you whether you know it or not. (6, 28, 34, 42 & 59)

(B). The Tao always existed and always will; something never born can never die. Those who allow their lives to be guided by the Tao are happy and fulfilled.(7)

(C). Keep your thought simple. Work at what you enjoy. Be truthful when speaking. Be honest when arguing. Be fair when making rules. Don't compare to others. Resist the urge to prove you are better than anybody else. (8)

(D). If you acquire more wealth than you need, the value of money will be lost. Wealth is no better than poverty. Fame is no better than ordinary life. Money and popularity do not bring happiness or fulfillment. Be satisfied with what you have, and what you have will bring contentment. A contented person is never sad or disappointed. (9 & 44)

(E). Empty your mind of your thoughts and your heart will open up to all things and all people. (16)

(F). Good teachers are trusted because they place their trust in us; when their works is done they say nothing, allowing their students to feel proud and empowered by their achievements. (17)

(G). When you act with your heart, it is said that you are "following the Tao". When you act with your mind, "you are ignoring the Tao". Those who follow the Tao are filled with peace and happiness. But any attempt to explain or describe the Tao will be useless. People who understand the Tao do not talk about it. People who talk about it don't truly understand it. When you are in harmony with Tao, winning and losing do not really matter. Your anger is tamed. Your intellect is forgotten. You have got no point to prove. You have neither friends nor enemies. All people are treated the same. When you are at peace with yourself, others are at peace with you. This is the highest state of being. Chaos and conflicts are resolved with the heart, not with logic and rules. (18, 35 & 56)

(H). The Tao teaches us perfection. The perfect traveler has no destination but his adventures inspire a thousand stories. The perfect teacher has no lesson but his students master all subjects. The perfect ruler has no power but the people place their trust in his judgment. In each case they are defined not by who they are, or by what they do from day to day, but by their openness to all things, all people and all ideas. (27)

(I). The Tao is the source of all harmony. Striving for one extreme more than the other upsets the balance that brings us peace and brings harmony to the world. Within the Tao, you will see the connection of all things. And you will see harmony is fragile easily broken by greed and arrogance. (29 & 39)

(J). When presidents and kings follow the Tao, they rule without force. They understand that making unfair demands on the people is like swimming against the current in a river. The best leaders do not use laws to govern the people. The best parents do not shout and scream to discipline their children. Their ability appears effortless; and it is: they accomplish much by doing nothing. This is the practice of "non-doing". Great leaders achieve result but they do not boast about them; they lead but they do not conquer. When leaders are honest people are satisfied. When they are dishonest, people are angry and place their trust in others. When our leaders stray from their path, we see results: a few people are wealthy while the rest are poor; a few people are powerful while the rest have littled influence over how they are governed. (30, 53 & 58)

(K). Weapons are the tools of fear and hate. Those who follow the Tao will only use weapons in self-defence. When such force is needed, it is with sadness, and the conquered are treated with respect and dignity. (31)

(L). When you let yourself be with the Tao all that should be accomplished is completed without thought or effort. Actions come naturally. You may not know your destination, yet each step of the journey feels right, leading to a place that seems unknown and yet also familiar. If our leaders understood this lesson, all people they serve will be content, happy and living their lives exactly as they should be lived. They would be without desire, and they would be at peace. (37)

(M). Allow the Tao into your heart and it will never leave you. Peace and prosperity begins with one person and then moves to one family, and then to one neighbourhood, and then to one city, and then to one country. It will grow and grow. When we ignore the Tao, we replace it with our own ideas: laws, justice, morality, worship, faith. When people think they know the answer to a mystery, they close their mind to new ideas. When people accept one religion, beliefs in other religions cause arguments. The same is true of the Tao; when you think you understand it, the power is lost. In ancient times, people who follow the Tao set an example for others – in the way they live each day – but they did not teach. To know the Tao, you must stop to understand it. This is the cause of world's chaos and confusion. (38, 54 & 65)

(N). Avoiding trouble is much easier than recovering from a bad decision. Doing things correctly from beginning to end is far better than doing all over again after a careless mistake. Those who follow the Tao accomplish much in life because they focus on each step of the journey not the destination or the end result. Non-doing is what happens when we take one step at a time. (64)

(O). The greatest rules put the needs of others above their own. Their power is used only to remain a good and loyal servant to the people. This is why people trust and follow them. (66)

From the above-stated essence of Tao, we will notice that the Tao resembles the energy source or negative pressure originating in the primordial void of space mentioned earlier ruling the universe with Yin and Yang harmony or balance. The Yin and Yang harmony is akin to the force-field interactions that create matters and make things happen. Above all, there is a form (Yang) and substance (Yin) or intent and purpose relationship ruling the universe. The further discovery of the Exclusion Principle, which says that no two leptons of the same quantum state, may at the same time be at the same place, provides us with yet another vital evidence of such mind and matter relationship. Based on the Exclusion Principle, various molecules and compounds are formed serving meaningful life purposes as may be verified by an examination of the Periodic Table. Scientists have commented that without the Exlusion Principle, the universe would have become a rather boring place being made mostly of hydrogen-like masses. The underlying mind and matter or form and substance relationship can be further verified by a corresponding energy transfer upon change equivalent to the rest mass of force carrier particles exchanged.

Additionally, from the Einstein's energy-mass equation ($E=MC^{2)}$ and quantum mechanics ($E=hv$) themselves, energy exists in a continuum from potential to kinetic, light and thought with a force measured by the square of the speed and frequency of light. Hence light and thought have a bigger role to play in restoring the total energy content of the universe back to zero given its quantum power – square of the speed and frequency of light - that originated from the primordial void prior to the Big Bang. Hence there exist overwhelming scientific evidences showing that the universe is ruled by the following primary laws of nature :-

1. Existence of a potential energy source in the primordial void of space with a propensity to form mirror-image particles and anti-particles and matters and anti-matters from smaller elemental binary energy states of : [(+1) + (-1)] ; [(+1)(+1) + (-1)(-1) + (+1)(-1) + (-1)(+1)].
2. Alternations of energy in smaller binary elemental energy states ruling the universe and our lives such that the total energy content upon exchange of forces and fields always sums to zero state as may be represented by a power of nothingness : [(+1) + (-1)+ (+1)(+1) + (-1)(-1) + (+1)(-1) + (-1)(+1) = 0].

Whether scientists can or cannot prove that the potential energy or negative pressure of the primordial void is the source of energy giving rise to the universe with the above-stated primary energy laws by the causal Newtonian-Darwinian science the fact remains that our heart and mind are so functioning as energy alternating in elemental energy states. In fact by the laws of conservation of energy, pair production, and its reverse process - annihilation of mirror-image particles and anti-particles upon contact – there exist overwhelming scientific evidences showing that the negative pressure of the primordial void is the force or potential energy source giving rise to the birth of the universe. The mind and matter continuum is concurrent with the findings under the Standard Model namely that matter is made of two groups of energy building blocks. Electron, proton, neutron and neutrino along with other particles form one group (and engage in antisymmetric dance) while meson and photon of light (and form a symmetric dance) form another. One group alone cannot achieve this without the other. These two groups of building blocks interact on four levels to form different levels of mirror-image three-dimensional matter based on a phenomenon of attraction of the opposites of charge, electron spin and quantum states. The strong force, weak force, electromagnetic force, and the gravitational force interact with the respective fields existing between particles of nucleus. Three of the fundamental forces result from the exchange of force-carrier particles, which belong to a broader group called "bosons". Each fundamental force has its own corresponding boson – the strong force is carried by the "gluon", the electromagnetic force is carried by the "photon", and the "W and Z bosons" are responsible for the weak force. Although not found, the "graviton" should be the corresponding force-carrying particle of gravity.

Specifically, the further discovery of cosmic microwaves left behind in space from stage formation of different levels or generations of matter is yet another vital piece of evidence lending weight to the Big Bang theory.

In any event, out of practical necessity, we routinely execute our complex tasks in RDBM as objects defined by intent (form) and purpose (substance) relationships in accord with the above-stated binary energy laws as elaborated in the foregoing: $[0= (+1) + (-1) + (+1)(+1) + (-1)(-1) + (+1)(-1) + (-1)(+1)]$.

It may be asked at this point, why are scientists insisting that they can explain everything based on causal proofs? In this regard, as elaborated by Stephen R. Covey in his book "Seven Habits of Highly Effective People", as human being, we are often deluded by an innate mental paradigm that lands us in the wrong territories, missing the wood for the trees. In short, as human being, we are part of energy functioning in the existential realm; $[(+1)(-1) + (-1)(+1)]$. Being in such existential state, we could only sense things or occurrences with our sensorial organs like eyes, ears, touch, and sense of smell, transmitted through the executive function in the prefrontal lobe to be interpreted experentially affected by our human selfness. In other words, as human being, it is beyond human faculty to sense energy or the first-cause of the universe. Scientists clearly are not spared of the delusion attributable to their innate mental paradigm. On the other hand, based on Einstein's energy-mass equation and quantum mechanics and laws of conservation of energy, pair production, everything that exists is made of energy functioning in a continuum. Time a product of human existence does not play a part in the first cause of the universe. Light itself is heavy being part of energy and existence itself which is powered by energy measured by the square of constant speed and frequency of light. The latter are constants of nature and part of the first cause. Any object traveling beyond the speed and frequency of light assumed possible by relativist theorists would be a case of the laws of nature breaking down. Based on Einstein's energy-mass and quantum equations, light clearly plays a role in restoring the total energy content back to the zero state of the primordial void. Hence when we talk about change, we need to go back to the drawing board and re-consider past assumptions from the first cause – presence of a force or Tao to better understand the universe.

CHAPTER TWO
Systems and Practices

A research study conducted on 4,000 firms in Europe, the U.S. and Asia by Stanford University and the London School of Economics, has shown that successful companies are run on good management practices which have a significant impact on productivity. Additionally, Mark Thomas, Gary Miles and Peter Fisk have explained in their book "The Complete CEO" that chief executives of world's biggest public listed corporations shared some success factors including "high personal standards, simple principles, commonsense rules and an inexhaustible curiosity". These conclusions were reached from in-depth researches on how 1,000 leaders of the worlds's largest quoted companies manage their businesses over the period 1997-2005 by comparing the way these leaders ran their businesses with long-term performance.

Based on these authoritative surveys, productivity is therefore not something technical or mechanical. It is behavioral depending on how management and workforce interact with behavioral rules to add values to serve needs and expectations of customers in the market place in a social exchange. For convenience, we would call such solution rule-of-thumb servant leadership.

In this regard, Jack Welch the ex-CEO of General Electrics who has succeeded in the 1970s to build the company from a relatively modest entity into the biggest multi-industry corporations of the time, has advised: "no matter how big is our business or how deep is our pocket, we cannot afford to do everything to satisfy everyone. According to him, business is all about winning and winning has to be based on observance of a simple set of behavioural rules, namely: strong and dynamic mission statement, shared values, candour, differentiation and voice/dignity. Companies practicing rule-of-thumb servant leadership include: G.E. Allied Signal, Proctor and Gamble, Starbuck, Pratt and Pratt and Whitney and many more. These successful companies have achieved transformational changes by following human behavioural rules like servant leadership, training, commitment to execution and two-way value-adding interactions with their workforce.

From these surveys, we can see that relationships hold the key to change. In this regard, J. M. Juran widely noted as the father of quality management has postulated in his book : "Breakthrough Change" on a change and control relationship in management. Alfred Chandler has proposed a "structure follows strategy" dictum to get things done. Chester Barnard a chief executive, has proposed harnessing of social forces of organization as key to success. In this regard, Warren Buffett has pointed out thus: "Look at three things in a person. Intelligence, energy and integrity. If they don't have the last one, don't even bother with the first two." Bill Gates of Microsoft Corporation has advised: "When we show people the problems, and show them the solutions, they will be moved to act" Similarly Charles G. Koch of Koch Industry was able to translate abstract goals to easily-to-recall cost-capacity targets by virtue of inherent mind and matter relationships as elaborated in his book: "Science of Success". Hence based on authoritative surveys and practical experiences of successful chief executives like Welch, the primary secret of success can be summed up as rule-of-thumb leadership, building the foundation of integrity and trust, commitment to execution, training of and two-way interaction with the workforce to add values and to harness the social forces of organization in a social exchange. (see Table A below).

It is common knowledge that in business, we cannot afford to do everything or satisfy everyone. This means that we need to simplify tasks, set priority and strategies before we could fulfill relevant relationships mentioned in the foregoing. The primary relationship is behavioral. Our thought like light being another form of energy, it is logical to behave according to the Tao and Te higher order ruling the universe. However, the Tao cannot act alone. It needs to be supported by the Te, very much like forces cannot act alone and need to interact with the fields to form mirror-image matters and anti-matters. As explained in Sun Tzu Art of War (STAW) and Clausewitz's "On War", while warfare is under the control of central governmental authority (form), success in execution of warfare depends on generals' exercise of intuitions, insights and talent with breaking of orders from time to time. This is implicit in STAW's tenet: "Victorious warriors first win (intention or form) then go to war while defeated warriors go to war then seek to win" (method or substance). Following the bad experience from the Vietnam War, a war doctrine known as the Weinberg Doctrine was formulated to correct past mistakes. This doctrine was systematically applied in the Gulf War and Iraq Wars by the U.S. strongly supported by public opinions, leading to swift winning, reduced casualties and political closure. (read "Masters of War" by Michael I. Handel).

However, owing to selfness of human nature, as explained in Chapter One, people have been looking at things from an inside-out cognitive perception or perspective. The Total Quality Management (TQM) methodology is a system based on aspect of quality, needs and expectations of customers. The Six Sigma and Toyota Production System (TPS) are species of TQM based on perspective of skill training, continuous improvements, people development and problem-solving skills. In fact TPS has its origin in the Training Within Industries Program (TWI), a skill training program commissioned by the US Department of War, designed with the objective to cope with the shortage of skilled workers during the war years in WWWII of 1940-1945. This TWI consists of 10-hour Sessions as follows:

1. Job Instruction (JI) - a course that taught trainers (supervisors and experienced workers) to train inexperienced workers faster. The instructors were taught to break down jobs into closely defined steps, show the procedures while explaining the key points and the reasons for the key points, then watch the student attempt under close coaching, and finally to gradually wean the student from the coaching. The course emphasized the credo, "If the worker hasn't learned, the instructor hasn't taught". At the request of enterprises outside of manufacturing, variations to the JI program were developed for hospitals, office and farms.

2. Job Methods (JM) - a course that taught workers to objectively evaluate the efficiency of their jobs and to methodically evaluate and suggest improvements. The course also worked with a job breakdown, but students were taught to analyze each step and determine if there were sufficient reason to continue to do it in that way by asking a series of pointed questions. If they determined some step could be done better by eliminating, combining, rearranging, or simplifying, they were to develop and apply the new method by selling it to the "boss" and co-workers, obtaining approval based on safety, quality, quantity, and cost, standardizing the new method, and giving credit.

3. Job Relations (JR) - a course that taught supervisors to deal with workers effectively and fairly. It emphasized the lesson, "People Must Be Treated As Individuals".

4. Program Development (PD) - the meta-course that taught those with responsibility for the training function to assist the line organization in solving production problems through training.

The TWI skill training program was introduced by Deming to Japan leading to its post-war rise as an economic powerhouse. It was further developed by Toyota into the 4-P (philosophy, people, process and problem solving) people development philosophy coupled to the PDCA (planning, doing, checking and adjusting) known as Toyota Business Practice to train workers to attain problem-solving skills in eight-step pro-people processes (1. clarify problem versus ideal state, 2. break down the problem, 3. set the target, 4. root-cause analysis, 5. develop countermeasures, 6. see countermeasures through, 7. monitor both result and processes, 8. standardise processes and identify gap in next steps).

Hence, TPS needs to be further fine-tuned into a people-process problem-solving skill supported by routines or kata, the Japanese term adopted in training of martial art by blackbelt karate master. While the 4-P people-development philosophy, and the PDCA continuous improvement are logical to development of quality controls and development of problem-solving skills, it is not the be-all-and-end-all of productivity and change as not all tasks can be laid in continuous workflow processes to expose inherent problems.

Unfortunately management has been developed into a "management theory jungle" as Harold Koontz called it due to differences of perceptions or perspectives In this regard, we are reminded that even the highly logical "one-best-fit" scientific method originated by Frederic Taylor widely acknowledged as the father of scientific management, has ended in dismal industrial dispute with the workforce.

In fact, Deng Xiao Peng has transformed China by basically observing such relational behavioural rules e.g. "modernization of China", "whether a cat is a black or white cat, it should catch mice", and "selfless leadership" which truly inspire his countrymen to work together bringing about transformational change for the common good based on integrity and trust. This is in deep contrast to China's five thousand years of centric emperorship, and Mao Tse-Tung's command and control approach which ended up as "flogging the dead horse". It is an undeniable fact by observing basic behavioural rules e.g. selflessness, strong mission, value-adding and motivation of people, Deng has succeeded in inspiring billions of Chinese into putting their innate talent to work raising standards of living for the ordinary citizens never enjoyed for the past five thousand years under centric emperorship.

Based on past experiences, the greatest obstacle to change is selfness of human nature. To avoid the common mistake of being trapped by the selfness of human nature, in OSP, we execute core tasks in form (Yang) and substance (Yin) relationships as follows:-

BASIC BEHAVIOURAL RULES OF RULE-OF-THUMB SERVANT LEADERSHIP
• Observing basic behavioural rules essential to building of integrity and trust, supported by form (intent) and substance (purpose) execution,
• Leading by servant leaderships, training of the workforce.
• Adding values with customer-centric focus.
• Mind and matter relationships.
• Setting priority and strategies to leverage on resource, application of knowledge, developing culture of creativity and innovation,

• Rule-of-thumb checklist supervision at two points – decision making and payment.
• Thinking and acting in oneness with the force within us that helps us change.

Table A – Fundamental relationships pertaining to productivity.

Hence based on our extensive review of past wisdom, experiences supported by ample scientific evidences, the universe is made of energy interacting via forces and fields in a continuum. Being energy, and part of nature, it is only logical that we need to work with the force or Tao according to the binary laws of energy. Out of practical necessity, in RDBM, we routinely executed tasks no matter how complex as objects defined by functions and values to better realise our goals and dreams.

CHAPTER THREE
Form and Substance Execution

We have in Chapters One and Two extensively reviewed past wisdom, experiences supported by ample scientific evidences that all things are energy alternating in smaller binary elemental energy states with a power to restore total energy content back to zero state of the primordial void upon change. Our thought being another form of energy, it is only logical that it functions in accord with such binary energy laws. Out of practical necessity, we routinely execute our tasks in relational database system (RDBM) as objects defined by binary intent (form) and purpose (substance) relationships.

As elaborated in Chapter Two, authoritative surveys, we have further shown that successful companies, have been following a rule-of-thumb servant leadership approach based on commitment to execution, and observing of basic behavioural rules to add values to the enterprise in a social exchange. (see Table A of Chapter Two)

In a nutshell, in OSP, such rule-of-thumb servant leadership is supported by relational database execution platform where we prototype, simulate and break down tasks to expose relationships which we fulfill via form (intent) and substance (purpose) execution as follows:-

> Tasks => 3 steps of administration + 10 specializations => core tasks => expose relationships => form and substance processing (to add values) => form processes (actions) => work-form processes (databases) => Setting strategies and KPI variances => results witnessed by facts

and data through rule-of-thumb checklist supervison monitored by the standard 4-part feedback task_lines.

On such concrete form and substance execution platform, we are able to avoid selfness of human nature and enable and empower all to work as a team to work productively by simple fundamental relationships as shown below:-

1. Administration, (form or intention) – we simplify and standardise tasks of administration into three steps namely: (a) studies of ideas, (b) making enquiries on resources, (c) securing of contracts as set up in forms (actions) and work_ forms (database).

2. Operations, (substance or method) - two-way form and substance execution of decisions in ten interrelated standard departments focused on adding values to products and services to serve customers' needs and expectations. Each department is focused on 2-4 core tasks executed to attain easy-to-recall targets set in forms (actions) and work_forms (database).

A practical example, would perhaps demonstrate how to make decisions and execute them productively on such administrative-operational framework without distractions from diverse concepts and theories, procrastinations or delays. As a common saying goes, the most important factors in business are namely: location, location and location. As highlighted by Lockyer in his book "Factory and Production Management" the management has to determine such location based on a diversity of complex issues as follows:-

1. Integration with other group companies
2. Availability of labour
3. Availability of housing
4. Availability of amenties
5. Availability of transport
6. Availability of materials
7. Availability of car parking space

8. Adequacy of circulation
9. Availability of services
10. Suitability of land and climate
11. Local building and planning regulations
12. Room for expansion
13. Safety requirements
14. Site cost
15. Political situation
16. Special grants.

Clearly, in making decisions on investments, there is a wide range of unknown, requiring exercise of intuitions, insight or experience. As shown in the afore-stated OSP processing flowchart, by laying bare workflow processes, in three steps of administration and ten departments of operation, we are exposing underlying intent and purpose, or form and substance relationships to facilitate execution. The primary relationship is building of integrity and trust. Although we cannot see our thought, or how it works, we instinctively are able to balance the Yin and Yang elements willy-nilly based on facts and data produced from inspections, and KPI strategies, easily monitored by the standard URL-like 4-part task-lines as shown below:-

1. idea-study-1.4.1.0-general/checklist_locational_factors_(1.4.2.0)/0
2. enquiry-resource- 2.4.1.0-general/NPV_IRR_cost_capacity_(2.4.2.0)/0
3. investment-contract-3.4.1.0-general/checklist_cost_capacity_target_(3.4.2.0)/0
4. invoice-accounts-4.1.3.0- accounts/ROI_checklist__expenditure_(4.1.2.0)/0
5. process-enforcement– 4.2.1.0-HR/Residual_site_cost_checklist_(4.7.3.0)/0
6. after_sale-facility-4.3.1.0-facility/warranty_checklist_ (4.3.2.1)/0
7. file-general-4.4.3.0-production/schedule _file_list_KPI_(4.4.3.0_ 4.7.4.0)/0
8. appraisal-HR-4.5.3.0 -production/osp_processing_test_(4.7.3.0_ 4.2.1.0)/0
9. sale-marketing-4.6.1.1-marketing/cost_capacity_value_adding_price_ volume_(4.6.2.1)/0
10. leveraging-material_4.7.1.0-production/capacity_cost _function _value_(4.7.2.0)/0
11. items_regulation-4.8.1.0 -regulations/laws_checklist_work_form_(4.8.2.0)/0
12. project-investment-4.9.1.0- revenue/NPV_IRR_form_(4.9.2.0)/0
13. service-security-4.10_2.1.0- service/patrol_checklist_form_(4.10_2.2.0)/0

The most unique feature of OSP is its 4-part standard task_line as shown in the foregoing, to enable the management to interact with the workforce as highlighted in the afore-elaborated workflow processes. It consists of: part-1: name, part-2: subname (attributes) part-3: task_ code and part-4 which is subdivided into three sub-parts being (a) department (b) facts and data complete with KPI (c) statuses ("0" for variant, "1" for closed). Parts 1 and 2 are jointly provided to give a brief, flexible yet comprehensive description of task proper so as to capture all issues/problems. Part 3 contains the coordinting reference task_code to link up all core tasks by systemic relationships.

Hence, in administration, we fulfill relationships set in 1-2-3 steps – study of ideas, enquiring on resource and securing of contracts - supported by facts and data e.g. investment returns, costs of transportations, and availability of material, labour, etc (see ID_1_ agenda and ER_1_quotation in Table B of Appendix I). In operation, we fulfill technical/operational relationships set in forms and work_ forms as stated in part-4 (sub-part-2) of task_line: e.g. (1.4.2.0), (2.4.2.0), (4.4.1.0_4.5.3.0), (4.4.3.0_4.7.4.0) (see Appendix I: core_task cards ID_ 2_data, ER_2_data, GE_1_supervision, HR_3_salary, HR_3_salary, PN_4_project).

In making "yes/no" complex investments, we exercise intuitions, insights or experiences from rule-of-thumb checklists (see Table A of Chapter Two). At the decision making level, we therefore balance the Tao (form) and Te (substance) with setting of priority, and strategies to leverage on resource and knowledge application as stated in the STAW tenet : "Victorious warriors first win (intention or form) then go to war while defeated warriors go to war then seek to win" (method or substance).

In operation, we expose the diversity of functions and values and fulfill them through form and substance execution. Part 4 sets priority and strategies relevant to particular circumstances upon facts and data generated by respective KPIs (bracketed sub-part-2 of part 4 of task-lines) focusing on the most significant factors or relationships (yes/no decisions based on facts/data generated by checklists/KPIs within forms and work_forms).

Coincidentally the core tasks of OSP can be aptly represented by the 52 normal playing card as explained in "Productivity Training Kit cum Business Strategy Card Game (OBS) (see Appendix I). With regular practice, of this entertaining OBS, it is possible to internalise workflow processes as an integral part of personal competency of the average

"Joe" to develop a culture of creativity and innovation for long-term sustainable growth.

The alternative to rule-of-thumb servant leadership would be add hoc, fire-fight practices or top-down command and control methodology distracted by all sorts of abstract concepts and theories including the following:-

1. Passion and persistence,
2. Proactivity,
3. Discipline,
4. Synthesis,
5. Creativity,
6. Respectfulness,
7. Ethical values,
8. Beginning with the end in mind,
9. First thing first,
10. Think win/win,
11. Seek to understand, then to be understood,
12. Quality, timeliness and cost effectiveness,
13. Set team rather than individual goals
14. Provide regular feedback on team performance to members,
15. Synergise,
16. Sharpen the saw,
17. When the going get tough, the tough get going,
18. Quitter never wins, winner never quits,
19. The key to developing people is to catch them doing the right things,
20. People who feel good about themselves produce good result etc etc.

Hundreds of ideas called impactful ideas are regularly featured in the media, self-help books and management/research journals such as the Harvard Business Journal etc. This is compounded by a jungle of concepts out there produced by the avalanche of management and self-help books. These concepts and theories are often abstract, and overlapping or repetitious, saying the same thing in different ways due to differences of perspectives or perceptions. For decades various management practitioners have noted that the common intuitive top-down command and control system has failed to work and called for change.

There is no doubt as Welch has highlighted in his book "Winning", we need to set priority and apply strategies, in order to focus on adding values, through leveraging of valuable resource and knowledge applications. In "Trading From Your Gut, (page 20), Curtis Faith related an incident showing how intuitions, insights and experiences play a critical part in such a research and development process. He highlighted that the whole world had been inflicted with a deadly virus called Polio back in 1908. Most of the researchers had been working on vaccines that used live viruses. They did not believe that dead viruses could be effective. The trials for live-virus vaccines proved dangerous because they infected the subjects with the very disease they were trying to innoculate against. Why did Jonus Salk decide to buck the trend and use the dead-virus vaccine when this approach had never been used. It all started with his intuition – a feeling that something just didn't make sense. That intuition had been acquired in his earlier years while learning about immunizing against diphtheria or tetenous bacteria. Salk's intuition paid off. His vaccine worked. Hundreds of thousands of people were saved from contracting polio because of his intuition.

As well pointed out by Peter Sander in his book "What would Steve Jobs do", there is a contention between the market-driven (money) and product-driven (or value_innovation) model taking place in developing of Apple Company as a world's leading computer manufacturer. At the time, the Chief Executive John Scurry preferred to run Apple on a market-driven model in sharp contrast to Steve's Product-driven (innovation-driven) model. This conflict led to departure of Steve for some eleven years. Upon Steve's return to head the company, he disclosed in a testimony for the 1995 Smithsonian Awards Program, that Apple had declined during the period 1985-1996 not due to company's rapid growth but a fundamental shift in values from a product-driven to a money-driven one. The rest was history as Steve brought Apple based on his product-driven philosophy once again as the number one computer maker of the world.

Hence, based on our review, quality control is not the be-all-end-all of productivity or change. Other important criteria include exercise of intuition, insight and experiences. Through form (intent) and substance (method) execution, we are able to expose relationships so as to think and act in oneness with the primary energy laws of Tao and Te higher order, witnessed by facts and data.

Under OSP, therefore, the Production Department of a research organization will be able to focus on core tasks of leveraging on material, equipment and scheduling of manufacturing processes taking advantage of changing commodity prices in the market place. The Marketing Department will focus on the 4-P (product, price, place and promotion) of marketing; the Facility Departments will render support to production and general departments in serving customers and supporting maintenance/operation of installations and equipment. The Service Department will harness the social forces in the external environment based on behavioural hands-on checklist supervision. The security guards provided by external agencies can be better treated as if they are part of staff and be motivated and trained, to attain easy-to-recall targets, willingly as stated in acronym: M.I.S.T.A.K.E. signifying compliance of targets set on (m)isuse of facility, (i)ntruder, (s)tealing, (t)raffic control, (a)lteration works, (k)ontractor activities and (e)errors. The character or reliability of the guards may be set at a high standard of discipline easily recalled by the acronym "C.I.D.S.H.O.P" signifying courtesy, integrity, discipline, smartly dressed, obedience, and punctuality. The Revenue Department will coordinate with Accounts and others to maximise on revenue investments and recovery of debts. The Regulation/Compliance Department ensures compliance of laws and regulations via processing of task-lines to preempt problems instead of waiting for problems to arise.

The Facility Department staff can be trained on form and substance execution to ensure that installations and facilities are inspected based on cyclical inspection to attain easy-to-recall targets. For example, it could set the fire-safety targets easily recalled by the acronym e.g. FIRE-SAVE-HANDLE standing for "fire alarm", "ringing bell", "smoke detector", "voice system", "handling (air)", "notifying", "door-closer", "lift-homing". Similarly, by rule-of-thumb checklist supervision, the management is able to monitor equipment/facility performance according to easy-to-recall targets e.g.: "(B)ody, (E)lement, (Starter), (T)orque and (P)arts".The Service (Cleaning) Department can easily monitore simple core tasks of (a) (C)leaning and (b) (C)hemical/ mechanical applications. Further, performances can be quantified as "1", "2" "3" signifying failed(33.33%)/ pass(66.67%)/ excellent (100%) respectively convertible to percentage moving averages used for month-end project certification of payment rather than relying on intuitive or ad hoc reporting. Based on weekly update/closing of variances based on cyclical inspections of defects, top management is able to maintain hands-on control over maintenance/operation of installations and operations of production equipment and machinery, electrical supplies, pumps, lifts, structural components of buildings etc.

In running of public services like the mass transit trains, bus, air travel, marine vessels, we have witnessed once too often, assortments of systems of look-good standards, codes and standard operating procedures under the control of laws and professional practices. However, such assortments often ended up as ad hoc fault-finding, pressure-cooker tactics or marchiavellian talk-only rhetorics (see PN_1_material and PN_3_equipment in Table B of Appendix I). The real test of talent and ability clearly lies in how the top management is able to motivate peoples, to work together to add values based on rule-of-thumb servant leadership, observing of strong mission, candour and shared values supported by cyclical inspection, correcting and preempting defects, if they hope to achieve breakthrough change. The political upheavals, and violent revolutions afflicting peoples and nations at large from antiquity are attributable to inefficiencies and malpractices with peoples in authority over-relying on from rather than substance such as laws, concepts and theories which have failed to work. Therefore, as stated at the outset, we need to tackle problems at the root. To be productive, we need to work towards balancing the form and substance. The OSP rule-of-thumb servant leadership is a form supported by the substance of an effective execution platform. OSP provides an opportunity for peoples and nations to work together to add values in win-win solution in a social exchange. To begin, just adopt servant leadership, supported by RDBM execution platform with observing of simple behavioural rules and values implemented in a rule-of-thumb checklist supervision.

By virtue of its robustness, OSP can be easily acquired with practice of OBS as stated in STAW's tenet: "Victorious warriors first win then go to war while defeated warriors go to war then seek to win". The Enforcement Department will conduct quarterly passing of OBS Tests. Through form and substance strategy the workforce is able to internalise easy-to-recall targets set in acronyms as an integral part of personal competency of the average "Joe".

At this point, we are once again reminded by the famous advice of Mark Twain: "The secret of getting ahead is to get started; the secret of getting started is breaking your complex and overwhelming tasks in small manageable tasks and then starting on the first one."

Therefore, as stated at the outset, whether you are a housewife, student, worker, boss, chief executive or governmental minister, you can make the difference. Be positive. Lead by servant leadership supported by rule-of-thumb checklist supervision and form and substance execution via weekly closing/updating of status signified by "0" (non-compliant) or "1" (completion) as shown in part 3 of task-line. Above all, be totally committed to execution in order to reap the fullest benefits of change. Any half-hearted effort is doomed to fail. By ready to collaborate with a hidden force, or Tao within our being. More importantly, just do it. Mankind has the luxury of time once of waiting for two thousand years before reaping the fruit of the atomism approach. The survival of mankind on this planet depends on such true leadership and meritocracy. It is not too late to start working with a force within our being for peace, harmony and progress. Considering that the road to change remains long and winding and the rife among peoples and nations are getting much serious with passing days with likelihood of erupting into nuclear wars that may wipe out the human race, there is no luxury of time. It would be counter-productive to continue dabbling in concepts like leadership, meritocracy, transparency and codes of good corporate governance, passion, persistence, perseverance consistency and focus as has happened for many decades now without making headway. The worse is doing nothing, compromising, procrastination and falling back on selfness, relying on propaganda and justifications to get by or seeking refuge in comfort zone. Above all, as the title of this book says: change, just do it. Supported by an effective relational execution platform as explained in details in Appendix I, you may now truly lead by servant leadership to work with a force within our being in a win-win situation witnessed by facts and data in a social exchange.

APPENDIX I
OSP Productivity Training Kit

This Appendix consists of two parts namely: (1) Productivity Training Kit and (2) OSP Business Strategy (OBS) Card/Mahjong Game. It is based on the Objective-Steps Processing (OSP) a relational database execution process that helps people work productively to realise their goals and dreams as explained in the productivity handbook "Change you can".

In a nutshell, in OSP, complex tasks are reduced by means of the outside-in atomism approach to smaller elemental core tasks to facilitate execution in form (intent) and substance (purpose) relationships. Coincidentally its core tasks are laid in 3 steps of administration and 10 departments of operations which can be aptly represented by the 52 normal playing cards/majong (though dedicated cards may be used with greater effect) as follows:-

THREE STEPS OF ADMINISTRATION:

Ideas – step 1 (1.4.n.0 -king)	Enquiries – step 2 (2.4.n.0-queen)	Contracts – step 3 (3.4.n.0- jack)
IDEA ID_1_agenda_1.4.1.0	*ENQUIRE RESOURCE* ER_1_quote_ 2.4.1.0	*Contract* CN_1_contract_3.4.1.0
IDEA ID_2_data_ 1.4.2.0	*ENQUIRE RESOURCE* ER_2_data_ 2.4.2.0	*Contract* CN_2_data_ 3.4.2.0
IDEA ID_3_matter_ arising_1.4.3.0	*ENQUIRE RESOURCE* ER_3_summary_2.4.3.0	*Contract* CN_3_signing_ 3.4.3.0
IDEA ID_4_ project_1.4.4.0	*CHECKLIST* ER_4_checklist_2.4.4.0	*CHECKLIST* CN_4_checklist_3.4.4.0

TEN AUTHENTIC INTERRELATED DEPARTMENTS OF OPERATION:-

Accounts_ dept_1 (4.1.n.0- Ace)	Enforcement_ dept_2 (4.2.n.0- Two)	Facility_dept_3 (4.3.n.0- Three)	General_dept_4 (4.4.n.0- Four)	HR_dept_5 (4.5.n.0- Five)
A ♠ *ACCOUNTS* AC_1_posting_ 4.1.1.0	**2** ♠ *ENFORCEMENT* EN_1_process_ 4.2.1.0	**3** ♠ *FACILITY* FA_1_customer_ 4.3.1.0	**4** ♠ *GENERAL* GE_1_supervision_ 4.4.1.0	**5** ♠ *HR* HR_1_recruitment_ 4.5.1.0
A ♥ *ACCOUNTS* AC_2_data_ 4.1.2.0	**2** ♥ *ENFORCEMENT* EN_2_data_ 4.2.2.0	**3** ♥ *FACILITY* FA_2_data_ 4.3.2.0	**4** ♥ *GENERAL* GE_2_data_ 4.4.2.0	**5** ♥ *HR* HR_2_data_ 4.5.2.0
A ♦ *ACCOUNTS* AC_3_invoice_ 4.1.3.0	**2** ♦ *CHECKLIST* EN_3_checklist_ 4.2.3.0	**3** ♦ *FACILITY* FA_3_equipment_ 4.3.3.0	**4** ♦ *GENERAL* GE_3_duty_ allocation_4.4.3.0	**5** ♦ *HR* HR_3_salary_ 4.5.3.0
A ♣ *ACCOUNTS* AC_4_journal_ 4.1.4.0	**2** ♣ *CHECKLIST* EN_4_checklist_ 4.2.4.0	**3** ♣ *CHECKLIST* FA_4_checklist_ 4.3.4.0	**4** ♣ *GENERAL* GE_4_ project_4.4.4.0	**5** ♣ *HR* HR_4_appraisal_ 4.5.4.0

Marketing_ dept_6 (4.6.n.0- six)	Production_ dept_7 (4.7.n.0- seven)	Regulation_ dept_8 (4.8.n.0- eight)	Revenue_dept_9 (4.9.n.0- nine)	Services_ dept_10 (4.10_n.n.0- ten)
6 ♠ MARKETING MK_1_4P_ 4.6.1.0	7 ♠ PRODUCTION PN_1_material_ 4.7.1.0	8 ♠ REGULATION RG_1_item_ 4.8.1.0	9 ♠ REVENUE RV_1_maximising_ 4.9.1.0	10 ♠ SERVICES SV_1_type_ _4.10_n.1.0
6 ♥ MARKETING MK_2_data_ 4.6.2.0	7 ♥ PRODUCTION PN_2_data_ 4.7.2.0	8 ♥ REGULATION RG_2_data_ 4.8.2.0	9 ♥ REVENUE RV_2_data_ 4.9.2.0	10 ♥ SERVICES SV_2_data_ 4.10_n.2.0
6 ♦ MARKETING MK_3_place_ 4.6.3.0	7 ♦ PRODUCTION PN_3_equipment_ 4.7.3.0	8 ♦ CHECKLIST RG_3_checklist_ 4.8.3.0	9 ♦ CHECKLIST RV_3_checklist_ 4.9.3.0	10 ♦ SERVICES SV_3_project _ 4.10 _n.3.0
6 ♣ MARKETING MK_4_project_ 4.6.4.0	7 ♣ PRODUCTION PN_4_schedule_ 4.7.4.0	8 ♣ CHECKLIST RG_4_checklist_ 4.8.4.0	9 ♣ CHECKLIST RV_4_checklist_ 4.9.4.0	10 ♣ CHECKLIST SV_4_checklist_ 4.10_n.4.0

Table B - OSP Diagram (core_tasks/checklists laid out in 3 steps and 10 depts)

Hence, with core tasks clearly identified, and connected in mind and matter relationships, as seen in Table B, tasks are no longer complex and uncertain. Because of its robustness, OSP is easily acquired with practice of OBS game. Therefore, this Appendix serves as an effective in-house productivity training program for the workforce as described by the rules of OBS below:

BASIC RULES OF OSP BUSINESS STRATEGY (OBS) CARD/MAJONG GAME

In this game, the King suit stands for the 1st step of administration, study of ideas which is subdivided into four core tasks namely: (1) agenda (2) database (3) matters arising and (4) projects signified by king of spade, heart, diamond and club respectively. The Queen suit, stands for the 2nd step, enquiring on resource. It is subdivided into four core tasks: (1) inviting quotation/submitting tender, (2) database (3) summary of quotations/tenders and (4) checklist signified by queen of spade, heart, diamond and club respectively. The Jack suit represents the third step namely securing of contracts which consists of core tasks: (1) tendering for contracts, (2) database (3) closing of contracts and (4) checklist supervision. The fourth step represents operation which is sub-divided into ten standard functional departments. For example, the Accounts department, the first operation department consists of four core tasks: (1) 4.1.1.0 : posting of transactions (2) 4.1.2.0: account statement (3) 4.1.3.0: invoicing payable/receivable and (4) 4.1.4.0: journal adjustments in that order signified by ace of spade, heart, diamond and club respectively. As can be seen from Table B, the other nine operation departments are subdivided into 2-4 core tasks each connected to systemic task_code relationships. e.g. 1.4.1.0, 2.4.1.0, 3.4.1.0, 4.1.1.0 etc etc.

A minimum of two with a maximum of four persons may take part in the OBS Card Game/Test. The cards are shuffled. Each player picks a card from the top of the shuffled deck, the highest card being spade of King, followed by its heart, diamond and club then by spade and heart etc of Queen similar to the rule in contract bridge game. The person picking the highest card will begin the play. The order of play is clockwise, to the left of person who has just played.

The immediate objective of the game is to draw and hold on-hand one core_task (or checklist card) card for each of 13 suits, (the complete array of cards) the soonest possible whereupon the player will declare "win" or "game" to win the game. The first player to do so wins the game and is awarded a game bonus of 20 points. The exciting part of the game is not winning but winning with the highest possible "off-hand" points obtained from playing two strategies as described below. In the event the last card of one pack is used up, a 2nd or even 3rd pack etc of cards may be shuffled and added to continue the play. The total number of points on-hand and "off-hand" (displayed on the OSP diagram) are added to the game bonus representing the total score won. Non-winners' scores will have their points (both on hand and in OSP diagram) disregarded.

In OSP, relationships hold the key to success. The principal relationships are behavioural that is servant leadership, commitment to execution, building of integrity and trust, observing of basic behavioural rules such as strong mission, values, candour and voice/dignity (as adopted by Welch of GE) essential to building of integrity and trust. These behavioural rules are fulfilled with rule-of-thumb checklist supervision and two-way form (intent) and substance (purpose) execution of core tasks. In this way, with practice of OBS card game, staff can be trained to balance the Tao and Te dualism to attain easy-to-recall targets set in forms and work_forms. In particular, they will learn that in whatever they are doing, one cannot be over-demanding, without rendering support to staff to make things work. This balance between Tao and Te is played out as witnessed by facts and data monitored by weekly updating/closure of statuses via the above-stated standard 4-part feedback task_line as detailed in Table C below:-

Code/ File	Department	Core tasks	Form (Actions)	Work_form (Database)	4-part Task-lines (last digit signifies status, "0" as undone, "1" as done)
1.1	Ideas	Agendas, Matter arising, Projects	1.4.1.0 1.4.3.0 1.4.4.0	1.4.2.0	idea-study-1.4.1.0-general /minutes_IRR_(1.4.2.0)/0
2.1	Enquiries	Tender/ quotations, summary	2.4.1.0 2.4.3.0	2.4.2.0	quote-resource-2.4.1.0-general/cost_ capacity_n_ (2.4.2.0)/0
3.1	Contracts	Negotiating contracts, projects	3.4.1.0 3.4.3.0	3.4.2.0	contract-piling-3.4.1.0-general/cost_capacity_ (3.4.3.0)/0
4.1	Accounts	Posting, Invoicing, Journal entries	4.1.1.0 4.1.3.0 4.1.4.0	4.1.2.0	invoicing-accounts-4.1.2.0-accounts/checklist_ (4.1.3.1)/0

Code/ File	Department	Core tasks	Form (Actions)	Work_form (Database)	4-part Task-lines (last digit signifies status, "0" as undone, "1" as done)
4.2	enforcement	processing	4.2.1.0	4.2.2.0	process-enforcement– 4.2.1.0-enforcement/ checklist_(4.7.3.0)/0
4.3	Facility	after_sale, equipment_ operation_ maintenance	4.3.1.0 4.3.3.0	4.3.2.0	after_sale-facility-4.3.1.0- facility/ vaccuum_ warranty_checklist_KPI_ (4.3.2.1)/0
4.4	General	overseeing, filing_ allocating_ duties, projects	4.4.1.0 4.4.3.0 4.4.4.0	4.4.2.0	file-general-4.4.3.0- production/schedule_ _ file_list_KPI_(4.4.3.0_ 4.7.4.0)/0
4.5	human_ resource	recruitment, career_ dev_ salary, appraisal,	4.5.1.0 4.5.3.0 4.5.4.0	4.5.2.0	salary_career_dev-HR- 4.5.3.0 -production/Mr._ X_core_tasks_ strategy_ test_(4.4-1.0_4.5.3.0)/0
4.6	Marketing	Price_ product, Place, Promotion,	4.6.1.0 4.6.3.0 4.6.4.0	4.6.2.0	4_p-marketing-4.6.1.1- marketing/cost_capacity_ value_ price_ volume_ (4.6.2.1)/1
4.7	production	Material, Equipment, Scheduling	4.7.1.0 4.7.3.0 4.7.4.0	4.7.2.0	leveraging-material_ 4.7.1.0- production/ items_n_cost_capacity_ value_ price_volume_ (4.7.2.0)/0
4.8	regulations	Items_ regulation	4.8.1.0	4.8.2.0	items_regulation- 4.8.1.0 -regulations/ laws_cases_checklist_ (4.8.2.0)/0
4.9	revenue	recovery_ investment	4.9.1.0	4.9.2.0	other_income- investment-4.9.1.0- revenue/NPV_KPI_ (4.9.1.0)/0
4.10_n	services	external_ services, project	4.10_n.1.1 4.10_n.3.1	4.10_n.2.0	service-security-4.10_ 1.1.0- service/patrol_ intruder_checklist_(4.10_ 1.2.0)/0

Table C – monitoring of performance via URL_like 4_part task_lines.

From Table C, we can see that the most unique feature of OSP is its two-tier short-rein monitoring of performance by the URL-like standard 4-part task_line to provide weekly feedback with closing/ updating of statuses. Just like the URL being constructed in sensor-datagram-network dot-separated relationships, is able to deliver great variety of messages to all corners of the globe at speed of light the 4-part standard task_line has rendered communication extraordinarily effective across the company. For instance, task_line : 1.4.1.0 (study of idea) consists of 4 digits. The first digit signifies the 1st step, the second digit signifies 4th department (general), the third digit stands for 1st core task and last digit "unfinished" ("0") status respectively. By way of another example, a task_line: 4.2.2.1 stands for 4th step (operation), 2nd department (enforcement), 2nd core_task (database), and "done" ("1") status. By weekly updating/closing of statuses denoted as "0" (open) or "1" (unfinished) the company is imbued with a sense of direction, timeliness and positivity towards attaining goals and dreams. Hence, the compact four-part URL-like task_line offers a two-way Tao and Te interactions between the management and workforce. It consists namely: part-1 the "step" [e.g. 1st, 2nd, 3rd step (administration) or 4th step (operation)]. Part-2: the department [e.g. department 1 (accounts), 2 (enforcement), 3(facility), 4 (general) etc.]. Part-3: the task_codes. Part-4: three sub-parts that provides facts and data supported by KPI set in forms and work_forms. The company is then able to monitor the facts and data generated by processing particularly as shown in sub-part-2 of part-4 of the task_line, via the task_codes of respective forms and work_forms. For example, KPI: (4.4.1.0_4.5.3.0) signifies the balancing of Yin and Yang elements in checklist supervision of staff's career development based on a force functioning within our being.

As elaborated in OSP form and substance flowchart, in Chapter Three, our thought as energy functions in alternations of binary (intent and purpose) elemental energy relationships within our being supported by 2-tier forms (workflow processes) and work_forms (database). Intent (Tao) alone is not enough. It needs to be complemented by relational execution (Te) based on a strategy of leveraging on resource and applications of knowledge. With balance of Tao and Te dualism our mind will follow through by doing the necessary and possible at the right place, time and in the right context by relationships.

The OBS is played in the following three modes:-

MODE ONE – ON_HAND CLOSING

A player who picks any core-task card e.g. 2.4.1.0, (spade of Queen) or 4.5.2.0 (heart of Five) may hold it on-hand without revealing it to earn one point or display it in the corresponding department box of the OSP diagram to earn two points. Any "checklist" card e.g. 4.2.3.0 (diamond of Two) signifying checklist supervision, may substitute for any core_task card in Mode One without any point scored. By playing in Mode One, a player aims to close the input boxes of the 13 suits the soonest possible. However, if he does so, he may miss opportunities to maximise his scores with the two strategies i.e. Mode-Two or Mode-Three as elaborated below.

MODE TWO - RESOURCE-LEVERAGING STRATEGY

Upon drawing of any royal-suit card i.e. King, Queen or Jack card, (1.4.n.n, 2.4.n.n, or 3.4.n.n) a player is deemed to be presented with an opportunity to leverage on resource. The royal suit resembles the owner/management board of a business. Given this opportunity, the player may instead of holding it "on_hand" to earn one point or display it in any of the ten department box of the OSP diagram to gain two points, place it in either the General (4.4.1.0) or Production box (4.7.1.0) of OSP diagram to be followed by subsequent placing of a core_task card of the "checked" Production/General box to gain a bonus of 8 points. As the game is played, the Enforcement Department's staff will be able to explain the values for each pairs so closed.

MODE THREE - KNOWLEDGE APPLICATION STRATEGY

A player drawing a "checklist" card, (signifying checklist supervision) may hold it on_hand (with no point added) or display it in any of the ten operational department boxes of the OSP diagram followed by subsequent placing of a core-task card of that "checked" box to do a pair-closing. The General Department being the supervisory department, its four core_task cards (4.4.1.0, 4.4.2.0, 4.4.3.0 and 4.4.4.0) may be used as wild card to substitute for any core_task card in performing the "checklist" pair_closing. Bonus points for "checklist" pair-closing are computed incementally as:[(checklist)+(any one core_task/wild card):4 points], [(checklist)+(any two contiguous core_task/wild cards):8 points], [(checklist)+(any three contiguous core_task/wild cards): 16 points], or [(checklist)+(four core_task/wild cards): 32 points].

A total of five games is played and the total scores added up and divided by five to obtain the average score. An appropriate criterion for passing of OBS test like 15 points (this may vary depending on experience) may be adopted. Hence, based on the OBS Card Game, the Enforcement Department staff is able to train staff on: (1) Functionality of core tasks, (2) Interrelationships to be fulfilled among core tasks (3) Setting of priority and strategy to leverage on resource and knowledge application and (4) Adding of values from fulfilling of KPIs set and (5) Two-way form and substance interactions between management and workforce to build integrity and trust.

A new staff is granted a total of three to six months to pass the in-house training ending with taking of the OBS test. The length of training depends on situations and needs. The training program is designed not to test the technical competency but rather to build a strong foundation of integrity and trust. The primary relationship is behavioural aimed at developing a culture of creativity and innovation for long-term sustainable growth of the whole enterprise.

SAMPLE FORMS AND WORK_FORMS

In OSP, the principal strategy adopted for rule-of-thumb servant leadership is checklist supervision, building of integrity and trust, and observing of basic behavioural rules to enable staff to attain easy-to-recall targets set in forms and work_forms. Confirmation of appointment, (4.5.1.0) salary increment, and promotion (4.5.3.0) and appraisal (4.5.4.0) are no longer ad hoc depending on personal opinions of supervisory personnel but is supported by passing of processing methodology (e.g. pair-closing of core tasks between Enforcement and HR departments) essential to building of integrity and trust, passing of strategy test verified by the MR database on performance. Hence, the HR will be truly transparent and objective by focusing on its four core tasks - recruitment, database, career-development-remuneration and appraisal – that truly motivate staff by two-way interactions, and observing of behaviours set in missions, values, candour and respect for voice/dignity to develop a competitive, creative and innovative workforce. A production department staff can be trained (e.g. 4.4.1.0_checklist_4.7.1.0) as elaborated in Mode Two or Three to leverage on resource or application of knowledge. A quarterly/half-yearly refresher training session and/or OBS strategy test may be held to enhance the competency in processing methodology and development of a culture of creativity and innovation for long-term sustainable growth as explained in "Change you can".

With weekly submission/updating/closing of statuses stated in last sub-part of part-4 of feedback task_line as recorded in the Management Report (MR) the company attains a sense of direction, consistency and focus, and in addition, timeliness essential to productivity and success. To illustrate the two-way interactions, for example, the production department staff may submit a task_line 4.7.1.0 indicating a proposal to leverage on dropping material prices in market place. The management may respond to such task_line input, 4.7.1.0 by specifying a relevant KPI (task_codes bracketed) in sub-part-2 of part-4 of task-line e.g. 4.7.2.0 prior to making a decision. Through such two-way interactions, the staff of production department may be motivated to be creative and innovative to seize opportunity to leverage on the drop in material prices. In the next weekly MR submission, the production staff update/close the task_line with relevant facts/data e.g. 4.7.2.1_4.4.1.1 indicating a positive database update or approval by the general department.

The sensitive information relating to prices of tender, costs of materials, and rental etc reported under the three steps of administration e.g. 1.4.1.0, 2.4.1.0 or 3.4.1.0 (see MR below) are kept under confidential files (not displayed) made available only to the CEO/key departmental heads. Guided by systemic task_codes, staff will be guided by coordination of functional tasks and tracing of any file, record, document, or investment/technical details via weekly submission of task_lines. All variances marked with "0" for last digit in part_3 (task_code) signify "unfinished" or "open" status which will be closed by changing the "0" to "1" upon complying with KPI by weeking updating/ closing of status every Friday.

The MR may be set up on Microsoft Access or MYSQL_PHP, to allow the whole of company to interact instantaneously. The MR may be displayed at the inner part of general office of each department to enable staff to update/close status on weekly basis by 3.00 pm on Friday.

The following are samples of Forms and Work_forms provided to illustrate the simplifying and standardizing of workflow processes. However, the actual forms and work_forms to be used will have to be based on individual circumstances. Rest assured that the structure of RDBM as explained remains unaffected.

SAMPLE OF FORMS AND WORK_FORMS

FORM
(2.4.1.0_enquiry_quotation_invitation: ref_2.4.1_1_of_4)

You are cordially invited to submit your quotation/tender for the works/ services/ supplies stated below to our office by hand (or by fax/post/ email when allowed) by the latest 12.00 noon of _____ (date) under confidentially sealed envelop marked with work reference no. stated on top left-hand corner of the envelop to be deposited into the tender box at the office.

The scope of work is:_____
(work reference no.:) as illustrated in attached layout plan A. All works/ services/supplies are to be executed and completed according to the quantity, quality and specifications as stated in Appendix I within a period of _____ days (inclusive of Sundays/Public holidays) from the date of commencement or issuing of purchase order. You are required to attend a show-round meeting at _____ am/pm on _____ (date) . Failure to attend the showround may disqualify you from participation.

FORM
(2.4.3.0_enquiry_summary:ref_2.4.3_3_of_4)

S/No.	Name (companies)	Subname (amounts)	Task_ code	Dept/facts_data_KPI/ status(0_1)
1	ABC	$nnn	2.4.3.0	production/quotation_ reinforcement_rods_1_ to_3_of_6 summary_ checklist_ (2.4.2.0)/0
2	DEF	$mmm		
3	XYZ	$kkk		
4	tanalised_piling	$qqq	4.6.3.0	mkg/tender_client_ site_ start_date/0

Evaluation Report by: _____

Decision of management: _____

NB:Workflow processes: (1) A minimum of three quotations is required from qualified and competent parties. Exception is to be supported by facts/data (2) A summary of quotations (for public services) complete with evaluation report is to be submitted for decision, and displayed on prominent notice board unless otherwise directed (3) Staff/members of board are to declare potential conflicts of interests (4) Terms/ conditions, scopes and specifications and description of works/services are to be clearly spelt out in invitation document. (5) Maintain updated catalogues, brochures to update clients.

WORK_FORM
(2.4.2.0_enquiry: ref_2.4.2_2_of_4))

ID	Dept_ID	Cat_ID	Name	Description	task_code	dept/facts_data_kpi/status
1	1	1	tender bid	piling_ tanalised_ X	2.4.1.0	mkg/$130,000_ start_ date_03_23_ 15_(4.6.1.0) /0
2	3	1	Quotation_ summary_3_ of_6 invitees	reinforced_rods_ 12mm_dia_ awarded_ABC_ $nnn_start _ date 04_ 16_15	2.4.3.0	production/ evaluation_ meeting_03_25_15_ (4.7.2.0_4.4.1.0) /0

WORK_FORM
(4.4.2.0_database_general_financial:ref_4.4.2_4_of_4))

S/NO.	NAME(CASH/ CHEQUE)	SUBNAME	Task_ code	dept/facts_data_kpi/ status
03/01/15	$1,000.00	$1,000.00	4.1.3.0	general/cash_petty_top_ up/0
03/13/15	-$45.00	$955.00	4.1.3.0	gen/petty_cash_DEF_ balance /0
03/14/15	-$32.00	$918.00	4.1.3.0	gen/petty cash refreshment: GHI
03/16/15	$560.00		4.6.1.0	Gen/sale_item_ /0
03/17/15	-$560.00		4.1.3.0	Gen/bank_in_03_17_15/0

NB:Workflow Processes: (1) Daily & monthly collection reports, cash variances, substantiated by pre-declared collection amounts, audit_roll, and bank_in, every Wed. (2) Submit cash balance records substantiated by facts and data to accounts department monthly by 3rd day of following month on variances, bank_in. (3) task_codes will provide facts and data to assist the accounts staff with proper posting of transactions.

FORM
(3.4.1.0_contract_tender: ref_3.4.1_1_of_4))

You are cordially invited to attend our special promotion/events_____
_____ to be held on _____ at _____. Discounts of up to
30% are being offered to our special customers like yourself. You may
fax/post/email your acceptance of our invitation to attend this event by
the latest 12.00 noon of _____

The highlight of promotion/even is :_____

NB:Workflow processes: (1) Invitations for promotion/events at quarterly
interval (2) Regular trade/project participations to establish common
interests with customers and community.

FORM
(3.4.3.0_contract_tender_submission/negotiation: ref_3.4.3_3_of_4)

S/No.	Name	Subname	Task_code	dept/facts_data_kpi/ status
1	piling_ tanalised_ site	contract	3.4.1.0	mkg/start_06_16_15_end_ 08_15_15_ tanalised_piling_ XYZ_tender_ $245,000_final $240,000.00/ 0

NB:Workflow processes: (1) Summary of tenders submitted is kept on
all tendering for projects (2) This form is used for updating of company
track record as shown in 3.4.2.0 below.

WORK_FORM
(3.4.2.0_database_contract: ref_3.4.2_2_of_4)

ID	Dept_ID	Cat_ID	Name	Subname	task_code	facts_data_kpi/status
1	2	1	tanalised_piling_site	contract	3.4.1.0	mkg/$240,000_start_06_16_15_end_08_15_15_client_X _site_Y_(4.7.1.0_4.6.1.0)/0
3	3	1	rc_piling_site	contract	3.4.3.0	mkg/$380,000.00_client_R_site_S_start_03_16_15_end _08_16_15_ (4.7.3.0_4.6.1.0) /0

FORM
(4.5.1.0_4.5.3.0_4.5.4.0_hr_recruitment_salary_appraisal: ref_4.5.n_1_of_6)

ID	Dept_ID	Cat_ID	Name	Description	Task_code	fact_data_kpi/ status
1	1	1	Recruitment	civil_engineer_xyz	4.5.1.0	prod/checklist_duties_osp_test_17pt_salary_$2,200_pm_wef_ 03_17_15_(4.5.2.0)/0
	3	1	salary_career_dev	civil_engineer_xyz		prod/osp_test_18pt_promotion_senior_engineer_ $3,000pm_wef_09_17_15_(4.5.2.0)/0
2	3	1	salary_career_dev	lmn_accounts_executive	4.5.3.0	acc/osp_test__18pt_form_ salary_$2,400_pm_wef_09_18_15_(4.5.2.0)/0
3	4	1	appraisal	def_marketing_executive	4.5.4.0	mkg/osp_test_18pt_form_ salary_$1,800pm_wef_08_16_15_(4.5.4.0)/0

NB:Workflow processes: (1) clearance by general dept: (2) verify duties, qualifications, title/salary/roster /date for position, (3) date/interviews/ shortlist (4) selection_approval, (5) appointment_ letter/ photo/ certificates/immediate_supervisor/ access_card /keys/ bank_account/ stationery/ software/ properties (6) notify accounts for salary_payment. (7) notify Enforcement for training and passing of Business Strategy test.

WORK_FORM
(4.5.2.0_database_hr: ref_4.5.2_2_of_6)

Date	Name	subname	task_code	dept/data_kpi/0
03/12/15	xyz	civil engineer	4.5.2.0	prod/ost_test_17_pt_ $2,200.00_ wef_03_17_15_ (4.4.1.1)/0
09/10/15	xyz	senior_ engineer	4.5.3.0	prod/promoted_osp_test_ 18pt_ $3,000.00_wef_09_17_15_ (4.4.1.1)/0
09/12/15	lmn	Accounts_ executive	4.5.3.0	acc/$2,400_wef_09_18_15_ osp_ test_18_pt_ (4.4.1.0)/0

WORK_FORM
(4.5.2.0_database_hr_financial:ref_4.5.2_3_of_6)

Date	Cash	Cheque	Task_code	KPI_balance_ diff_account_ head_ bank-in
03/01/15	$200.00		4.1.3.0	hr/$200.00_petty_cash_ top-up cheque/0
03/04/15	-$45.00		4.1.3.0	hr/$155.00_balance_ Robertteh_ stationery/0
03.06/15		-S$349.00	4.5.3.0	hr/salary_ refund_ex_staff_ bcd/0

NB:Workflow Processes: (1) Update collection/balance weekly by Wed (2) Submit records to accounts department monthly by 3rd day of following month on variances, bank_in.

FORM
(4.5.1.0_hr_recruitment_appointment:ref_4.5.1_4_of_6)

POST OF _____

We refer to your recent interview for the above-mentioned position at our office on _____. We are pleased to offer you the appointment on the following terms and conditions:-

1. Salary: $_____ per calendar month (CPF payable by employee will be deducted from this sum) with effect from _____.
2. Duties and responsibilities: _____
   Your immediate supervisor is _____.
3. The appointment is subject to confirmation upon passing of in-house training, and strategy competency tests within a probationary period of three months.
4. You shall carry out duties and responsibilities diligently and comply with company's policies, and instructions of supervisorsory officers and standing orders.
5. Both parties reserve the right to serve a one-month notice after confirmation of appointment to terminate the appointment without assigning of any reason whatsoever. During the probationary period, the notice period for termination is 7 days. Such notice period shall be inclusive of Sundays and Public holidays.
6. Company reserves the right to terminate the service of the employee without any notice at any time upon breach of conduct, e.g. leakage of company's commercial secrets to external parties, disobeying of instructions of supervisors, engagement in activities prejudicial to the interests of the company.

NB:Workflow processes: (1) Verify labour laws, collective agreement, contributions, (2) interview and decisions by heads/panel (3) check qualifications/experiences with source (4) arrange processing methodology/strategy test (5) accounts/departments notified.

FORM
(4.5.3.0_hr_career development_salary: ref_4.5.3_5_of_6_form_to_be_ appended)

NB:Workflow Processes: (1) Review manpower structure bi-annually in consultation with General Department (2) Review records of OSP_ methodology and strategy tests (3) Review appraisal database from MR.

FORM
(4.5.4.0_hr_appraisal: ref_4.5.4_6_of_6_form_to_be_appended)

NB:Workflow Processes: (1) Submit appraisal_form (4.5.4_4_of_4) twice per annum, (2) verify performance data and fact from MR (4.4.1.0)

FORM
(4.3.1.0_4.3.3.0_facility: ref_4.3.n_1_of_3)

ID	Dept_ID	Cat_ID	Name	Description	Task_ code	fact_data_kpi/ status
1	1	1	customer service_ after_ sale	facility	4.3.1.0	facility/checklist_ B.E.S.T.P _customer_ID_ defects_ warranty_exp_ 03_17_16/0
2	3	1	Installations_ maintenance	facility	4.3.3.0	production/checklist_ B.E.S.T.P_switchgear_09_ 18_16/0

NB:Workflow processes: (1) Verify terms and conditions, warranty (2) checklist_items (3) test_reading_variances (4) accounts_invoices/ departments notified.

WORK_FORM
(4.3.2.0_facility: ref_4.3.2_2_of_3)

ID	Dept_ID	Cat_ID	Name	Description	Task_code	fact_data_kpi/ status
1	1	1	customer_ID	defect_warranty	4.3.1.0	facility/client_C_site_D_ checklist_B.E.S.T.P_ warranty_exp_03_17_16_ (4.3.2.0_ 4.6.1.0)/0
2	2	1	Installations _item _x	cyclical_inspection	4.3.3.0	accounts/claim_repair_ warranty_exp_03_18_ 16_ B.E.S.T.P_(4.1.3.0_ 4.3.3.0)/0

WORK_FORM
(4.3.2.0_facility_financial: 4.3.2_3_of_3)

Date	Cash	Cheque	Task_code	Diff, details, Bank-in
03/01/15	$200.00		4.1.1.0	Top-up cheque
03/03/15	-$65.00		4.3.3.0	Robertteh; stationery

NB:Workflow Processes: (1) Prepare cash balance weekly by Wed (2) Submit cash balance records to accounts department monthly by 3rd day of following month on variances, bank_in.

FORM
(1.4.1.0_general_agenda: ref_1.4.1_2_of_4_sample_to_be_appended)

NB:Workflow processes: (1) check compliance with regulations on notice, quorum and display and monthly/annual meeting dates (2) set easy-to-recall month_end or periodic date (3) include mandatory_ financial items of agenda.

FORM
(1.4.3.0_general_matter_arising:ref_1.4.3_3_of_4_sample_to_appended)

NB:Workflow processes: (1) delegations and status (2) progress reports.

WORK_FORM
(1.4.2.0_general_minutes_notes_1.4.2_4_of_4_sample_to_be_appended)

NB:Workflow processes: (1) minutes confirmation/update (2) display_ circulation dates.

MANAGEMENT REPORT
4.4.1.0 (general_checklist_supervision:ref_4.4.1_1_of_4)

Name	Sub-name	Task_ code	dept/KPI_data/status_0_or_1
Quotation_ summary	reinforcement_ rods_12mm_dia	2.4.3.0	production/closing_19_3_ 15_summary_1_to_3_of_6_ attached_ confidential/0
tender_ piling_ tanalised	client_X_site_Y	3.4.1.0	marketing/$245,000.00_closing_ 03_19_15_ start_05_16_15_end_ 07_16_15_confidential/0
contract_rc_ piling	client_R_site_S	3.4.3.0	marketing/$380,000.00_start_ 06_16_15_end_ 08_16_15_ confidential/0
Recruitment	civil_ engineer_ xyz	4.5.1.0	hr/$2,200.00pm_start_03_09_15_ osp_test_17pt _(4.5.1.0_4.4.1.0)/0
salary_ career_ deve	civil_ engineer_ xyz	4.5.3.0	hr/promoted_$3,000.00_09_ 17_ 15_osp_test_18pt _(4.2.1.0 _ 4.4.1.0)/0
recruitment	accounts_ exe_ lmn	4.5.1.0	hr/$2,400.00pm_09_18_15_osp_ 18pt_(4.2.1.0_ 4.4.1.0)/0
appraisal	marketing_ exe_ def	4.5.4.0	hr/osp_test_17pt_$1,800.00pm_ 08_16_15_ (4.2.1.0_4.6.2.0)/0

Name	Sub-name	Task_code	dept/KPI_data/status_0_or_1
after_sale	warranty_repairs	4.3.1.0	facility/client_C_site_D_checklist_B.E.S.T.P_ 03_17_15_(4.3.2.0_4.6.1.0)/0
cyclical_inspection	installation_item _x	4.3.3.0	facility/claim_warranty_exp_09_18_16_checklist _B.E.S.T.P_(4.1.3.0_4.3.3.0)/0

WORKFLOW PROCESSES FOR ALL FORMS AND WORK_FORMS

NB: Workflow Processes: (1) Submit the standard task_lines to MR for variances/ exceptions/issues only (extracted from forms and work_forms) at weekly interval by Friday 3.00 pm. (2) Updating/closing of statuses is shown in last digit of part-3 : (e.g. substitute "0" by "1") witnessed by KPI facts/data from subpart-2 of part-4. (3) Forms and work_forms are serially collated e.g. 2.4.1_1_of_4 signifies document no.1 out of total of 4 forms/work_forms to avoid duplication/loss of records.

Printed in the United States
By Bookmasters